Good Habits to Have

Good Habits to Have

TRACY CAROL TAYLOR

PRINCE OF PAGES, INC.
ARLINGTON

Good Habits to Have

Copyright © 2019 All rights reserved.

No part of this book may be reproduced, scanned, or distributed in any printed or electronic form without permission. Please do not participate or encourage piracy of copyrighted materials in violation of the author's rights. Purchase only authorized editions.

Prince of Pages, Inc.

N. Carlin Springs Road. Arlington, VA 22203

www.princeofpages.com

ISBN: 9781949252279

Contents

	Introduction	1
1.	Be Proactive	3
2.	Spend Less Than You Earn	4
3.	Creator vs. Consumer	5
4.	Stay on Course	6
5.	Keep it Simple	7
6.	First Things First	8
7.	Beware Peer Pressure	9
8.	Make Today Your Best Day Ever	10
9.	Always Dress Your Best	11
10.	Seek Understanding	12
11.	Learn to Speak Properly and Clearly	13
12.	Learn Multiple Languages	14
13.	Learn to Successfully Run a Business	15
14.	Build an Emergency Fund	16
15.	Get Rid of High Interest Debts First	17
16.	Seek a Financial Advisor	18
17.	Learn to Really Listen	19
18.	Review Your Credit Report	20

19.	Read Every Day	21
20.	Buy Life Insurance	22
21.	Exercise Every Day	23
22.	Trim Your Bills	24
23.	Build Positive Relationships	25
24.	Set Big Goals	26
25.	Get a Good Night Sleep	27
26.	Develop Multiple Means of Income	28
27.	Learn to Forgive Others	29
28.	Renting vs. Owning: Which is Better?	30
29.	Avoid Wastes of Time	31
30.	Buy a Reliable Car	32
31.	Your First Car Should be a Used Car	33
32.	Drive the Speed Limit	34
33.	Maintain Good Health	35
34.	Invest in Energy Efficiency	36
35.	Give Generously to Those in Need	37
36.	Be a Good Neighbor	38
37.	Learn Kakeibo	39
38.	Enough is Enough	40
39.	Seek to Reduce High Interest Rates	41
40.	Learn to be Happy	42
41.	Be Smart About Personal Finances	43
42.	Small Beginnings	44
43.	Learn to Invest Wisely	45

44.	Learn Moderation	46
45.	Never Blame Others	47
46.	Stop Worrying	48
47.	Employer Matching Contributions	49
48.	Learn to Network	50
49.	Do You Really Need It?	51
50.	Make a Meal Plan	52
51.	Spend Less	53
52.	Plan Your Meals	54
53.	Active Income vs. Passive Income	55
54.	Grocery List are Good	56
55.	Specific Goals and Big Ideas	57
56.	Never Go Shopping Hungry	58
57.	New, Bigger, and Better?	59
58.	Never Say "I Can't"	60
59.	Engage in Free Hobbies	61
60.	Never Stop Learning	62
61.	Learn to Recognize Your Thoughts	63
62.	Try Everything Once	64
63.	Make a List	65
64.	Don't Worry About What Others Do or Think	66
65.	Never Give Up	67
66.	Don't Worry About Other Peoples' Money	68
67.	Passive Income: Rental Property	69
68.	Forever Friends	70

69.	Learn from the Rich	71
70.	Know Your Interest Rates	72
71.	Pay Off Your Card at the End of the Month	73
72.	Always Read A Contract	74
73.	Review Your Career and Finances	75
74.	Get a Mentor	76
75.	Minimum Balance Plus Interest	77
76.	Cut Up Your Credit Cards	78
77.	Learn from Your Failures	79
78.	Use Time Wisely	80
79.	Take Personal Finance Classes	81
80.	Start a Side Business	82
81.	Be Positive	83
82.	Shop Small	84
83.	Never Ignore Your Bills	85
84.	Be Helpful	86
85.	Avoid Salt, Sugar, and Fat	87
86.	Be Thankful	88
87.	Use LED Lights	89
88.	Be a Volunteer	90
89.	Learn to Price Compare	91
90.	Be Gentle and Be Kind	92
91.	Fix It Yourself	93
92.	Learn Self Control	94
93.	Maintain Your Car	95

94.	Passive Income Ideas	96
95.	Avoid Negative People	97
96.	Don't Gamble	98
97.	Avoid Vice	99
98.	Don't be a Mouse/Couch Potato	100
99.	Learn to Use Debt Wisely	101
100.	Brown Bag Lunches	102
101.	Control Your Emotions	103
102.	Use Public Transportation	104
103.	Don't Make Rash Decisions	105
104.	Discuss Money and Dreams Together	106
105.	Set Goals, Not Wishes	107
106.	Use Money Orders to Pay Bills	108
107.	Avoid Procrastination	109
108.	Talk Less, Take Less, and Be More	110
109.	Purchase CDs. No Not Music.	111
110.	Trash vs. Treasure	112
111.	Don't Give Up	113
112.	Go to a 2-year College First	114
113.	Avoid Pity Parties	115
114.	Luck?	116
115.	Destiny and Purpose	117
116.	Seize the Day	118
117.	At Ease	119
118.	Know When to Say No	120

119.	Rest and Relax	121
120.	Manage Your Money	122
121.	Learn to Recognize Value	123
122.	Set Realistic Goals	124
123.	Avoid Bad Debts	125
124.	Good Debt vs. Bad Debt	126
125.	Be Patient	127
126.	Delay Gratification	128
127.	Assets vs. Liabilities	129
128.	Believe in Yourself	130
129.	Prepare to Start the Day	131
130.	Learn the Value of Lay-Away	132
131.	Time is Money. Use it Wisely.	133
132.	Learn to Think Properly	134
133.	Calculated Risks	135
134.	Meaning of Calculated Risk	136
135.	Spend Time with Your Family	137
136.	Retire or Not to Retire	138
137.	Learn Something New	139
138.	Audiobooks	140
139.	Don't Play the Lottery	141
140.	Learn to Take Good Care of Your Things	142
141.	Good Hygiene	143
142.	Virtues	144
143.	Money is a Tool	145

144.	Your Reputation	146
145.	Honesty	147
146.	Invest in Yourself	148
147.	Want vs. Need	149
148.	Plan for Your Vacations	150
149.	More Ways Than One	151
150.	Learn Leadership Skills	152
151.	Always Give Back	153
	Suggested Reading	155

The information in this book is good information that everyone should know. Unfortunately, this information is no longer taught in school and some people never find out this information until much later in life.

I have complied this information from personal experience and information I researched on the internet. I would advise everyone thirteen years old and up to read, heed, and plan for your financial future.

This book is a very basic and introductory information. More is always available for learning. I recommend taking personal financial classes to better educate yourself and your children. I also recommend taking business classes on how to properly run a business. That way no matter what happens, you will always know how to generate income; active or passive.

Knowledge is always the first step in freedom.

"Teach a man to fish and he will never go hungry."

1. Be Proactive

Be Proactive. Don't wait for things to get worse. Look for ways to head off trouble before it comes. Always seek ways to make things better. Read "Who Moved My Cheese" by Spencer Johnson.

2. Spend Less Than You Earn

Spend less than you earn. If you only make $1500, then do NOT spend $2000. You will never get out of the money pit that you have dug for yourself.

3. Creator vs. Consumer

Poor people are consumers. Rich people are creators. Rich people create content, products, and services that other people buy. That's how they get rich. Poor people will continue to buy and never learn to create. Think about all the things that you have. Who made it? Who are you giving your money to? And can you make something that other people will buy from you?

4. Stay on Course

Begin with the end in mind. Always make a plan and try to stick to it. However, do realize that things may change and that unplanned things do happen. Be flexible. But always remain on course.

5. Keep it Simple

Keep everything as simple as possible. Never try to get the most expensive of anything. Whether it is a house, a car, a watch, etc. The most basic will do its mission just fine, until you can afford to buy better with cash. Trying to keep up with the Jones without the Jones' money will only get you deeper and deeper into debt.

6. First Things First

Put first things first. Crawl before you walk. Walk before you Run. Don't try to build mountains, without first having built your molehills. Poor people try to skip to the end and gain it all. Rich people know that it takes time, money, and effort to make their dreams come true.

7. Beware Peer Pressure

Never let people talk you into doing something that you know is wrong. One, you will never get away unseen and two, you will most likely get stuck holding the bag. Good and honest people never have to worry about getting caught.

8. Make Today Your Best Day Ever

Never put off doing things today. Tomorrow may never come, or you may have other things to do. Meredith Wilson once said, "You pile up enough tomorrows, and you'll find you are left with nothing but a lot of empty yesterdays. I don't know about you, but I'd like to make today worth remembering.

9. Always Dress Your Best

Dress for success. Always wear your best. Even when you don't think your best is good enough. Take care of the way you look, but don't let it become an obsession. You don't need rich clothes to look good. Brush your teeth, wash your face, comb your hair, and iron your clothes. This will be a good start. People will always like well-dressed people.

10. Seek Understanding

Seek first to understand, then to be understood. Stop talking and learn to listen. When you understand, then you will not end up doing things twice and will limit your mistakes.

11. Learn to Speak Properly and Clearly

Learn to speak English properly. I don't mean just learning English, but learn elocution. This is true for any language actually. Take speech classes or hire a speaking coach. It is hard to understand people who do not speak clearly. So if you wish to be heard, speak up and speak clearly.

12. Learn Multiple Languages

Learn more than one language. People who know more than one language are more marketable and are more valuable as employees.

13. Learn to Successfully Run a Business

Take business classes and learn to properly run a business. If you can do this, then you will never be out of work no matter what the economy does. Because you will always know how to use your talents to make money.

14. Build an Emergency Fund

Focus first on building an emergency fund. Save any change that you have left at the end of the day in a piggy bank or jar. Then at the end of the month, take all that change to the bank and put it into a savings account and let it collect interest.

15. Get Rid of High Interest Debts First

Focus second on eliminating high-interest debt. Depending on the interest rate, you could end up paying way more than the amount of money that you owed.

16. Seek a Financial Advisor

Seek the help of a financial advisor in order to start saving for retirement. The earlier you start, the better off you will be.

17. Learn to Really Listen

Learn to Listen. Really listen. Too many people spend so much time talking, that they never learn anything. You have two ears, but only one mouth. You were designed that way for a reason.

18. Review Your Credit Report

At least once a year, get and review your credit report. Correct any wrong or incorrect information.

19. Read Every Day

Read every day. Wealthy people read biographies of other people and self-help books. They are always looking for ways to improve themselves.

20. Buy Life Insurance

Buy term life insurance to cover you and your dependents. You never know what may happen, and the unexpected can take you or your loved ones in an instant. Life Insurance will cover you for the financial burdens that may incur.

21. Exercise Every Day

Exercise (at least 30mins) every day. Physical exercise releases chemicals in the body that improve memory, energy, and well-being. Not to mention weight loss. A healthy body is a wealthy body.

22. Trim Your Bills

Cut the fat from every single one of your bills. If you're not using it, get rid of it or donate it to someone else.

23. Build Positive Relationships

Build Positive relationships. (1.) Friends should always be encouraging, positive, and supportive of each other. (2.) You will become like who you hang around with. Hang with negative people going nowhere and there you will be too.

24. Set Big Goals

Set big goals and keep reminding yourself of them.

25. Get a Good Night Sleep

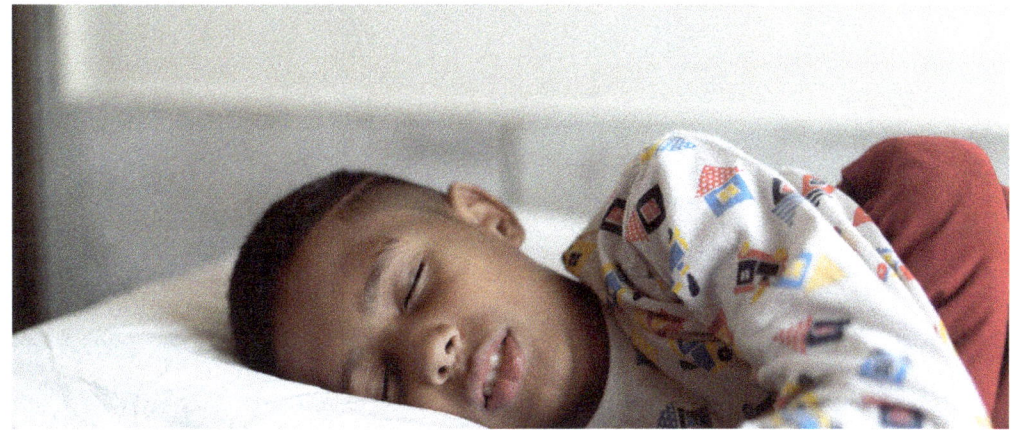

Sleep well and try to get at least 7 hours every night. Sleeping is just as important as exercising. Letting the mind and body rest, will renew you and give you means the tackle a new day.

26. Develop Multiple Means of Income

Develop multiple incomes. Rich people have at least three to seven means of income, both active and passive. Investments, Saving Plans, a 9-5 job, or even stocks and bonds.

27. Learn to Forgive Others

Learn to forgive. Learn to forgive your mistakes. Don't beat yourself up about them. You can't change them, so learn from them and then correct them. Also, learn to forgive others. Life is too short to waste time, energy, and money being mad. Besides, you'd want others to forgive you, right?

28. Renting vs. Owning: Which is Better?

Rent unless your total monthly cost of home ownership is lower than renting.

29. Avoid Wastes of Time

Avoid wastes of time. It is OK to relax sometimes. You mind and body will be better for it. However, you also need to spend your time doing productive things. Be they chores, taking classes, or even a creating things to sell. Learn to spend your time wisely.

30. Buy a Reliable Car

Buy cars based on reliability and fuel efficiency or buy a good used cars. Because cars loose value fast, sometimes it is better to buy good used cars than buy a brand new car.

31. Your First Car Should be a Used Car

Drive used cars – buy after depreciation and buy a luxury used car. No one will know that your Cadillac or Ferrari is used unless you tell them.

32. Drive the Speed Limit

Drive the speed limit. No sense giving money away in fines from tickets.

33. Maintain Good Health

Maintain physical and mental health. Nothing will kill you faster than poor health and stress.

34. Invest in Energy Efficiency

Air seal your home. Make sure you have good energy efficient windows and doors. Ultimately, they will save you money in heating and cooling your home.

35. Give Generously to Those in Need

Give money generously to charities. No one has ever lost out their reward on giving to those less fortunate. Kindness and Compassion that is given freely, will always return when you need it.

36. Be a Good Neighbor

Build strong relationships with your neighbors.

37. Learn Kakeibo

Make a budget and live within your means. Learn Kakeibo.

38. Enough is Enough

Learn when enough is enough. Holding onto things you don't need, and always wanting more, are the two biggest mistakes that people can make. Having too much stuff will clutter up your life and empty your wallet.

39. Seek to Reduce High Interest Rates

Request rate reductions on your debts, especially credit card debts.

40. Learn to be Happy

Learn that stuff doesn't make you happy. Stuff can be stolen, lost, or destroyed. Then you are sad. But if you can be happy just as you are, then no one can take your happiness.

41. Be Smart About Personal Finances

Teach your children about smart personal finance from day one and be a good example.

42. Small Beginnings

Save your change. Just as great trees grow from small acorns. So do millionaires from small beginnings and good investments.

43. Learn to Invest Wisely

Invest some of your money in stocks – and then hold on no matter what happens. Who knows how much money you'd have had if you hadn't dumped your IBM and Apple stocks long ago. At the same time, do realize when a ship is sinking and not coming back. Good financial wisdom is like poker, know when to hold them and know when to fold them. Stocks will always rise and fall. And it usually takes years for any stock to become a success. So be patient.

44. Learn Moderation

Learn Moderation. Too much of anything will make you sick, broke, or both.

45. Never Blame Others

Never blame other things or other people for your failures. Poor people shift blame. Rich people look for ways to learn from their failures and make plans to do better next time.

46. Stop Worrying

Stop worrying. Worry causes stress and stress makes you sick.

47. Employer Matching Contributions

Get every possible dime of employer matching in your 401(k) or 403(b).

48. Learn to Network

Never gossip, but learn to network. Every wealthy person has two to three people whose abilities complement their own. They may also have skills that you'd might like to learn.

49. Do You Really Need It?

Before you buy anything, ask yourself *'do I really need this'*? This one question will save you money and keep your life clutter free.

50. Make a Meal Plan

Make a meal plan at the start of each week. This can help you with keeping your shopping expenses low and will help you keep your weight under control.

51. Spend Less

Never spend what you earn, just because you can. Buying luxuries to look rich, will in the end, cause you to spend more and more money on useless things that you don't need. Learn to be happy with less.

52. Plan Your Meals

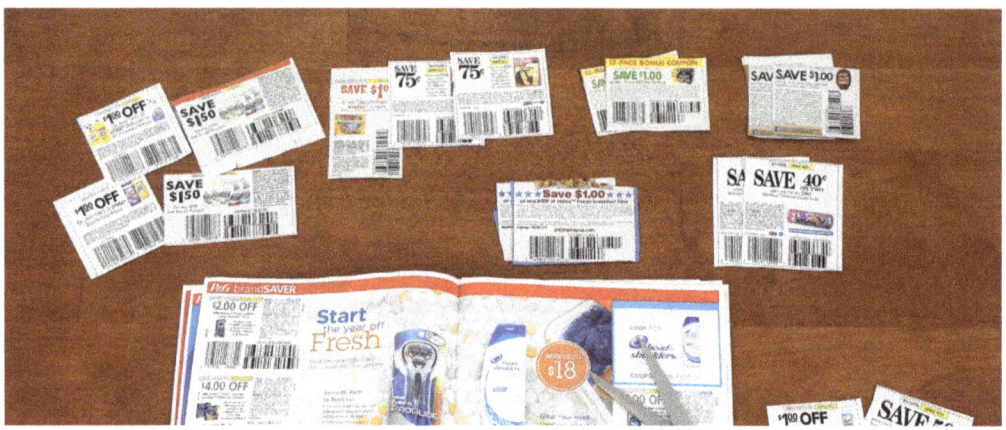

Use your grocery store flyer to assemble that meal plan.

53. Active Income vs. Passive Income

Learn the difference between active income, passive income, and capital gains.

54. Grocery List are Good

Don't ever go shopping without a grocery list. Without one you tend to buy things that you don't need, already have, or just plain want just because. Stick to the list.

55. Specific Goals and Big Ideas

You can have big ideas, just make sure you have specific goals that lead towards that dream.

56. Never Go Shopping Hungry

Never go shopping hungry and never make impulse purchases. If you're hungry and go shopping, you're more likely to overspend. If you're standing in line and waiting to pay, then don't just grab things you see. Impulse purchases are like little foxes and will spoil your wallet.

57. New, Bigger, and Better?

Ignore advertising for new, bigger, and better things. Learn that you have enough and that less means less bills to pay.

58. Never Say "I Can't"

Never say I can't. Always say I can, or I will someday.

59. Engage in Free Hobbies

Find hobbies that are free and don't require an upkeep cost.

60. Never Stop Learning

Never despise school. Wealthy people never stop learning.

61. Learn to Recognize Your Thoughts

Learn to recognize the thoughts that you have. Are they pushing you forward towards your dreams, or holding you back because of your fear? Fear of failing, fear of being laughed at, fear of not being good enough or that someone will do it better. Recognize your fear and then overcome it.

62. Try Everything Once

Try anything and everything that's free in your community.

63. Make a List

Make a checklist of things to do every day. Then cross them off as you complete them. Reward your achievements.

64. Don't Worry About What Others Do or Think

Don't worry about what other people do or think. You will stress yourself out or run yourself ragged trying to live up to or copy what other people do. Just be yourself and you'll be happier.

65. Never Give Up

Never give up when things get hard. Just keep Trying. Losers quit, but winners overcome. It's OK to admit that you don't know. That's one reason why we continue to learn and to grow.

66. Don't Worry About Other Peoples' Money

Don't worry about how other people spend their money. Jealousy will only make you mad and cause you to make bad decisions.

67. Passive Income: Rental Property

If you can afford to buy rental property, then do so and rent it out. This is known as passive income.

68. Forever Friends

Put in the time to build good, strong, lasting relationships.

69. Learn from the Rich

Hang around and learn from people richer than you. Learn how they manage their money. Learn how they save, and learn what they truly spend their money on.

70. Know Your Interest Rates

Always seek to know the interest rate of all loans, credit cards, and other debts. Never open credit cards with more than 10% interest on debt.

71. Pay Off Your Card at the End of the Month

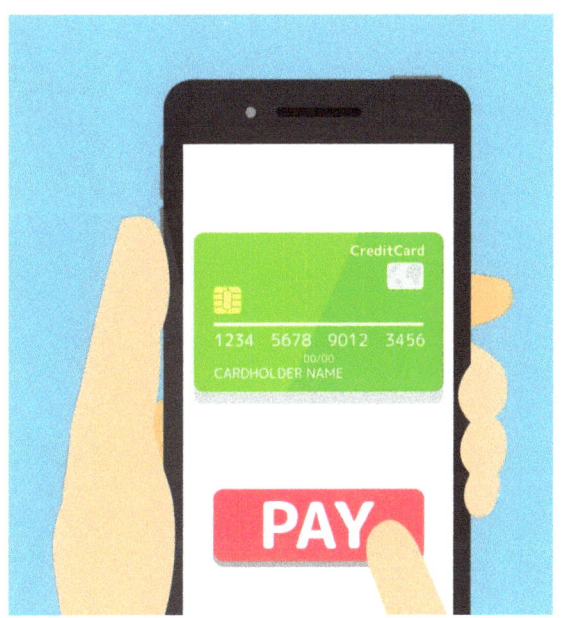

If you can, always pay off the full balance of a credit card by the end of the month to avoid paying interest rates.

72. Always Read A Contract

NEVER SIGN ANYTHING, BEFORE READING IT **ALL** FIRST. Always read letters, instructions, and contracts in full before giving your response. Many people have been tripped up by fine print.

73. Review Your Career and Finances

Review your finances, your career, and your life once a month. This will help you to see where you stand and then you can determine if you are still on track.

74. Get a Mentor

Get a mentor and/or become and apprentice to someone who has the skills that you want to learn.

75. Minimum Balance Plus Interest

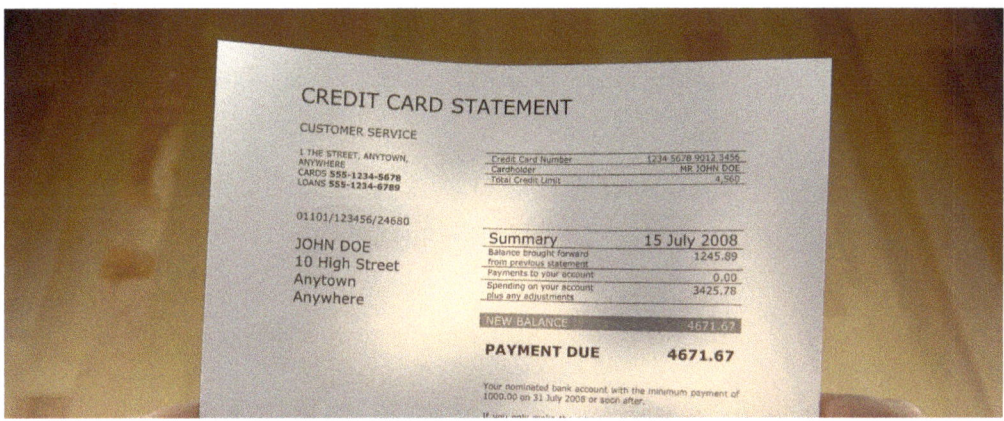

When paying your credit cards, always pay the minimum balance plus the interest, plus at least $50 dollars more. Otherwise, you will be paying more money than you ever owed.

76. Cut Up Your Credit Cards

Cut up credit cards that have high balances. That way you will not be tempted to use them again. Until they are completely paid in full. and do NOT close the card, this will be reflected negatively on your credit report.

77. Learn from Your Failures

Learn from every failure. Then get back up and try again.

78. Use Time Wisely

Find meaningful things to spend your spare time on. Do your hobbies bring you joy? Can your projects be sold to make you extra money and bring happiness to someone else?

79. Take Personal Finance Classes

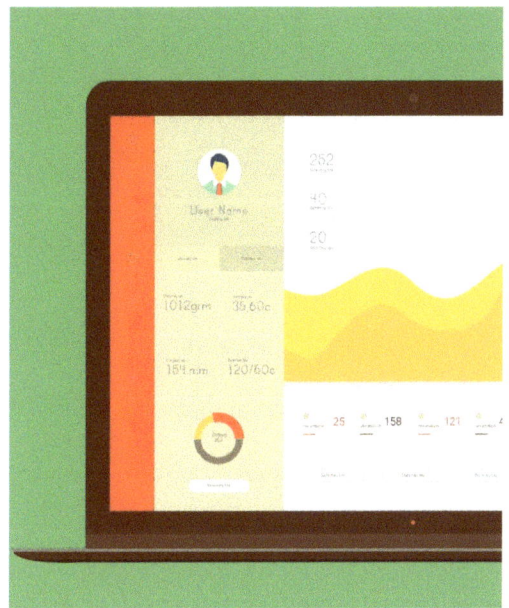

Take personal finance classes. Learn to properly manage your money. This will keep your from going completely broke.

80. Start a Side Business

Start a side business doing the thing you've always wanted to do. Do something you love and you'll never work a day.

81. Be Positive

Be positive. Keep an open mind and be up for new experiences.

82. Shop Small

If you're on a budget, shop first at the low-end stores. Remember that shopping local will not only help your community, but will keep the money in your community too. This will usually go to schools, roads, parks, and more.

83. Never Ignore Your Bills

Never just ignore your bills. If you can't pay them, call the company up and ask for more time; or work out a payment plan with them that works for you. Never just let them sit or throw them away. Avoiding a problem because you don't want to deal with it, won't make it go away. It will only make it worse.

84. Be Helpful

Always help others. Do a good deed every day.

85. Avoid Salt, Sugar, and Fat

Cut back on convenience foods. Sugar, salt, and fat are the enemies of a healthy body. In fact, read the ingredients of your food and find out what they do to the body. High Fructose Corn Syrup and sugar have been shown to drive inflammation, which is associated with an increased risk of obesity, diabetes, heart disease, and cancer.

86. Be Thankful

Be thankful. Nothing irritates people faster than dealing with people who are ungrateful and unthankful.

87. Use LED Lights

Use LED light bulbs. Using energy efficient equipment, will save you money in the long run.

88. Be a Volunteer

Volunteer. It's an easy way to meet new people, learn new things, and make new friends. Oh, yeah, and you'll be helping others.

89. Learn to Price Compare

If you're on a budget, Price-compare the grocery options in your area and choose the one with the best value. Cheap doesn't always mean better and pricey doesn't always mean good.

90. Be Gentle and Be Kind

Be gentle. There is no need for harsh words or harsh attitudes. Being Rich doesn't always mean in money. Some people are rich in friends or in attitude.

91. Fix It Yourself

When you have a problem, try to fix it yourself. Look it up on the internet or read a book. If it is an easy fix, do it yourself. If not, THEN hire a professional to fix the issue.

92. Learn Self Control

Learn self-control.

93. Maintain Your Car

Keep up with your car maintenance. Small problems cost less than small problems that were ignored and became costly problems.

94. Passive Income Ideas

Find a way to make more money. If you have a blog, a website, or even a podcast, then you can charge for your information and services and thus create passive income that you can earn whether you work on it or not.

95. Avoid Negative People

Avoid negative people. Negative people will always tell you no and find ways to waste your time. They always say, "I can't". Often they are going nowhere and want you to join them. Pity parties are the worse kinds of parties to throw.

96. Don't Gamble

Don't gamble. Now you're just giving money away and getting nothing but broke in return.

97. Avoid Vice

No smoking, no drinking, and no drugs. Wealthy people know that they need a clear head to make good decisions.

98. Don't be a Mouse/Couch Potato

Limit the time you watch TV and use the Internet. (don't be a mouse/couch potato).

99. Learn to Use Debt Wisely

Poor people take loans out for things that depreciate like cars, houses, boats, etc. Rich people take out loans for investing, growing a business that will make them more money, or education that will allow them to learn to make money. They get a return of investment on their loans.

100. Brown Bag Lunches

Eat leftovers and brown bag your lunches. This saves you money and provides you with good healthy food.

101. Control Your Emotions

Control your emotions. Bad emotions make bad decisions.

102. Use Public Transportation

Use public transportation, especially if it can help you to eliminate a car. Or invest in an e-bicycle. Cars are liabilities and an e-bicycle is an asset.

103. Don't Make Rash Decisions

Don't make rash decisions or take rash actions. Always take time to think about the consequences and repercussions. Will your decision add value to your life or make it worse?

104. Discuss Money and Dreams Together

Share your dreams and your mistakes with your partner; and then discuss solutions together.

105. Set Goals, Not Wishes

Set goals, not wishes. It's OK to wish for something, but it's even better to make a plan to make it happen.

106. Use Money Orders to Pay Bills

Use Money Orders not Checks. Once you write a check, you have no control over when it will come in. Sometimes, you write a check thinking that the money is gone and then write another one. Not realizing that the first check hasn't cleared yet and the second check you just wrote will bounce your account and cost you a fee. With money orders, once it's made out, the money is gone. And there will never be forgotten checks coming in or bad check fees.

107. Avoid Procrastination

Avoid procrastination. Unless, you are taking time to relax your mind and body, you can always be doing something to improve your lifestyle. Because putting things off until tomorrow will only add to your stress levels later.

108. Talk Less, Take Less, and Be More

Talk less and listen more. Take less and give more.

109. Purchase CDs. No Not Music.

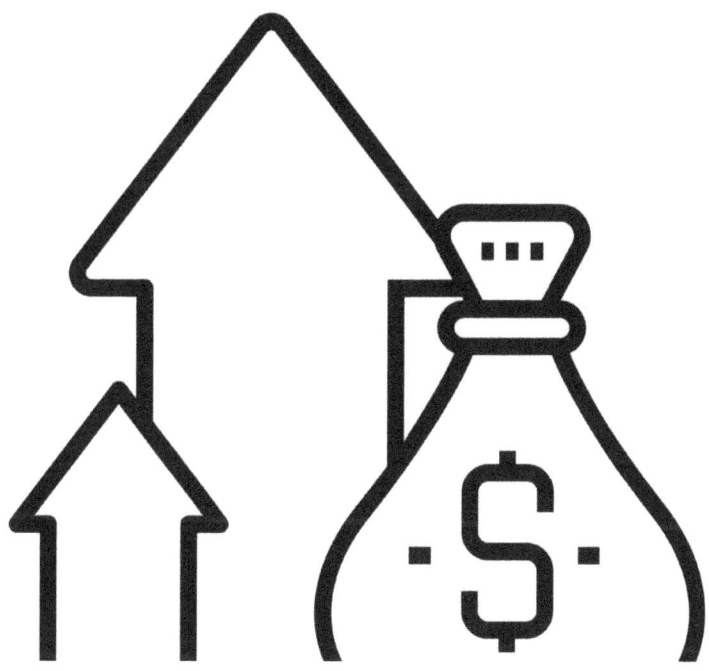

Get Certificates of Deposit (CDs) with a good interest rate. Saving little by little now, will give you more and more later on.

110. Trash vs. Treasure

Buy things at a thrift store, fix them up, and then sell it for more money.

111. Don't Give Up

Don't give up. Learning any skill masterfully will always take time, patience, and practice.

112. Go to a 2-year College First

Get your Math, History, English and other lower degree classes out of the way first by going to a cheaper 2-year college. These credits will not cost as much and will often transfer. Use a four year college to gain your higher degree classes. That way you can still say you graduated from a 4-year college, but will end up with only half the Student debt as if you took all your classes at the higher costing 4-year college.

113. Avoid Pity Parties

Set aside self-limiting beliefs. Wealthy people don't give up before they even try.

114. Luck?

Eliminate "bad luck" from your vocabulary. Luck vs. Skill. Poor people believe in luck. Rich people develop skills.

115. Destiny and Purpose

Know your main purpose. Some know, and that's all they want to be. Some don't know, and spend a lifetime looking for something. Whatever it is that you love to do, and would gladly spend your whole life doing, is probably what you're meant to do.

116. Seize the Day

Wake up early. Meditate, exercise, eat breakfast, and make a list. Start the day ready to face it. Go!

117. At Ease

Meditate. Rest your mind. Take time for you.

118. Know When to Say No

Know when to say no. Don't spread yourself too thin. And Don't be afraid to say no. Some people think that others will think less of them. Or that they have failed. But you need to know your limits; mentally as well as physically.

119. Rest and Relax

Rest, relax, refresh yourself. Take time off. Spend time with your family. That way, you won't have any regrets in the future.

120. Manage Your Money

Manage your money. Eliminate waste. (ie. Cancel unused memberships and subscriptions.)

121. Learn to Recognize Value

Learn to recognize the value of something. Ask yourself, does this object, person, or activity add value to my life? Can I reuse this again, or will I continue to use this? What do you get out of the things that you do? Is it enriching?

122. Set Realistic Goals

Set meaningful and realistic goals.

123. Avoid Bad Debts

Avoid Bad Debt. Don't fall for the credit card trap. Unless you are paying the minimum payment, plus the interest, plus at least $25 more, then you will never pay the card off.

124. Good Debt vs. Bad Debt

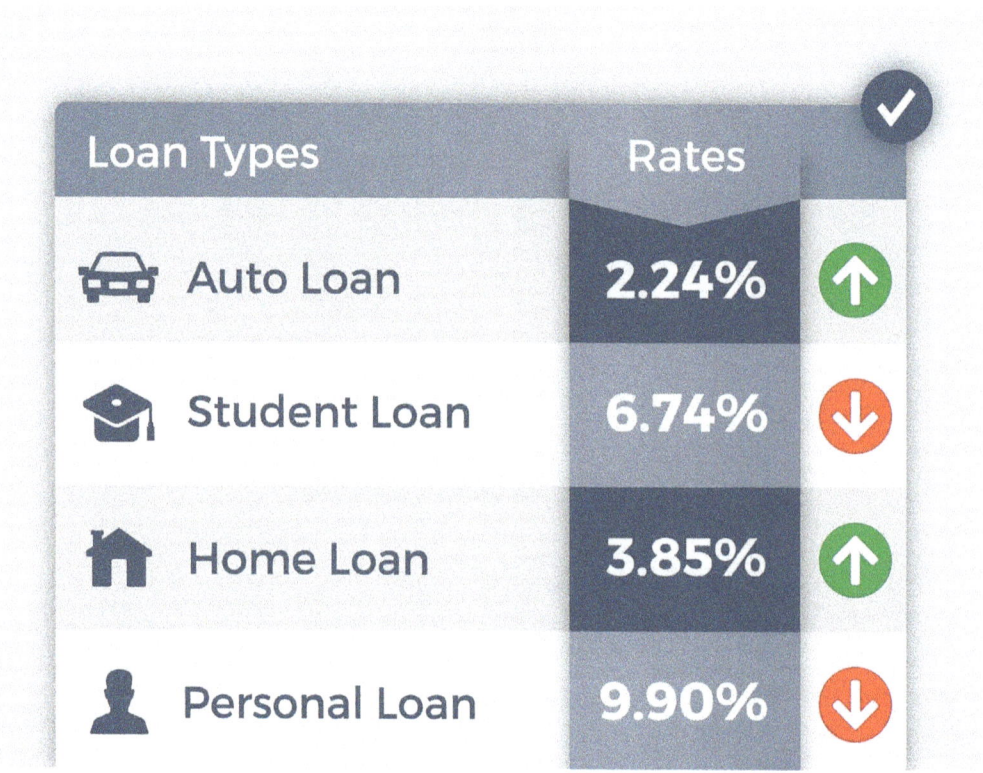

Learn the difference between Good debt and Bad debt.

125. Be Patient

Be patient. True wealth is accumulated a little at a time and day by day. Every day, put your spare change into a piggy bank. Then every month, calculate up all that you have saved and put it into a savings account with good interest.

126. Delay Gratification

Delay gratification (until you can pay for it in cash). Wealthy people know better than to pay for things with credit cards. They lay away money, little by little, until they can pay for it in full. Poor people want everything now. And thus, have lots of bad debt.

127. Assets vs. Liabilities

Learn the difference between assets and liabilities. Assets put money into your pocket. Liabilities take money out of your pocket. Houses, cars, boats, etc. are Liabilities. You're paying every month. Rental properties, stocks and bonds, and owning a business are all assets. You're getting paid every month.

128. Believe in Yourself

Believe in yourself. You can do anything that you put your mind to. It just takes time, knowledge, and determination. A might oak grows from a small acorn.

129. Prepare to Start the Day

Don't check your emails first thing. First, eat a good healthy breakfast, meditate, read your bible, or exercise. Prepare yourself to start the day.

130. Learn the Value of Lay-Away

Use lay-away, not credit cards. Delayed gratification will never come back later to bite you in the butt with hidden fees, interest rates, or debt collector calls.

131. Time is Money. Use it Wisely.

Believe that time is money. Don't waste money. Be constructive. Even when you are playing, you can learn new things. Playing house? Try practicing building one. Playing with legos? Learn construction or engineering.

132. Learn to Think Properly

Learn to think properly. Positive motivations, thoughts, and actions enrich not only you, but the people around you. Negative thoughts only hold you back and create negative feelings and emotions in you and in others.

133. Calculated Risks

Learn how to take calculated risks.

134. Meaning of Calculated Risk

Learn the meaning of calculated risk.

135. Spend Time with Your Family

Know when to stop working. Spend time with your family. Take time to listen to your children. They need your understanding and guidance too.

136. Retire or Not to Retire

Choose not to retire? Retire from your 9-5 job, but never stop learning or trying to earn a passive income to supplement your retirement.

137. Learn Something New

Challenge yourself to learn something new.

138. Audiobooks

Audiobooks. If you don't have time to read, then just listen. It will teach you to listen to others and understand them when they speak.

139. Don't Play the Lottery

Don't play the lottery. Invest your money in a savings account that gives good interest. Playing the lottery is giving away money that will never come back. Invested money is giving away money that will come back to you with interest.

140. Learn to Take Good Care of Your Things

Take good care of the things that you are given, or the things that you buy, and they will last a long long time.

141. Good Hygiene

Brush your teeth and always smile.

142. Virtues

Learn to be kind, considerate, and compassionate.

143. Money is a Tool

Learn that money is a resource and nothing else. It is a tool just like a shovel or a toaster. If you want to go farther than walking, then get a car or use the bus. If you want to fix something, then get a tool to fix it. Money is the same. What you can do, depends on what you have.

144. Your Reputation

Remember that your name will travel farther than you ever will. A good reputation is worth more than gold. Trust is never given, but earned. And even harder to regain once it is lost.

145. Honesty

Always be honest and trustworthy. If you give someone your word, then keep it.

146. Invest in Yourself

Learn that having nice stuff doesn't make you rich. It makes you poor. Rich people don't spend their money on stuff, but spend their money on investments, in themselves through education and in their businesses, by learning to make them better.

147. Want vs. Need

Learn to manage your money wisely. You don't need to buy everything you see.

148. Plan for Your Vacations

Plan for your vacations. Save up money in savings accounts that give good interest rates. So while you're saving up, you are also earning money.

149. More Ways One

Learn the different ways to earn money. There are more ways to earn money than just going to work at a job.

150. Learn Leadership Skills

Learn good social and leadership skills.

151. Always Give Back

Learn that the best way to make money is to help others. Find a problem and develop a solution. If you've ever seen SHARK TANK on TV. Then you've seen lots of people creating things that solve problems. So don't waste money on the lottery. Spend your time inventing something new or upgrading something that has already been invented.

Suggested Reading

"Who Moved My Cheese" by Spencer Johnson

Investopedia.com

"Fixing the Money Thing" by Gary Keesee

Motley Fool.com

"Rich Dad/Poor Dad" by Robert Kiyosaki

Alux.com

"The Millionaire Next Door" by Thomas Stanley and William Danko

"The Total Money Makeover" by Dave Ramsey

"Smart Women Finish Rich" by David Bach

"The Truth About Money" by Ric Edelman

"Broke Millennial: Stop Scraping By and Get Your Financial Life Together" by Erin Lowry

The Power of Habit: Why We Do What We Do in Life and Business, by Charles Duhigg

www.ingramcontent.com/pod-product-compliance
Lightning Source LLC
Chambersburg PA
CBHW041218240426
43661CB00012B/1080